MY
PRAYERS

Bethan James and
Krisztina Kallai Nagy

SCAMP.
PUBLISHING

Two little ears to hear with,
Two little eyes so I can see,
One little mouth and
one little nose,
Ten little fingers,
ten little toes,
Thank you, God,
for making me ME.

Thank you, God, that you made me
and that I am special to you.
Thank you, God, that you knew my
name even before I was born.
Thank you, God, that you love me,
just as I am.

5

Help us, Father God, to love each other,
to care for each other and to be
especially kind to each other today.

6

Thank you, God,
For people who love me,
For people who care for me,
For people who comfort me,
For people who help me,
Thank you, God,
For my family.

Thank you for being there, God,
when the sun rises in the morning.
Thank you for being there,
when the stars come out at night!
Thank you for loving me, God,
when I am happy and smiling,
or cross and grumpy,
or sad and lonely.
Thank you for always being there, God,
and for loving me.

8

Creator God who made me,
Creator God who loves me,
Creator God who cares for me,
Keep me safe today.

For this new morning and its light,
For rest and shelter of the night,
For health and food, for love and friends,
For every gift your goodness sends,
Thank you, gracious Lord.

O Lord God, how great you are!
When I look at the moon and the stars,
I feel so tiny,
I don't understand why you care about me.
O Lord God, how great you are!

O God, your generous love
surrounds us,
and everything we enjoy
comes from you.

God is great!
God is good!
Let us thank him
For our food.

All good gifts around us
Are sent from heaven above.
Then thank the Lord,
O thank the Lord,
For all his love.

13

Lord God, who never slumbers or sleeps,
bless us as we go out
and keep us safe as we return,
today and every day.

14

Father God, keep me in your care;
Father God, always be my friend;
Father God, guide me in everything I do.
Bless me now and protect me
until the end of my journey.

You, God, made sea and sand,
sun and snow, mountains and rivers
and hillsides. You made the big,
wide world and all the good things
that are in it.
You are amazing!

Your world is awesome, God!
Everything you made is beautiful.
Thank you that I am here to enjoy it.

17

Spotty ladybirds, stripy snails,
Butterflies and buzzing bees,
Slimy slugs with silvery trails,
Wiggly worms and centipedes,
Crawling creatures with long tails:
Thank you, God,
you made all these.

Splashy sea,
Big blue sky,
Shiny stones,
Grasses tall.
Trickling sand,
Knobbly shells...
Thank you, God!
You made it all.

Thank you, God,
for creatures great and small:
for ears on donkeys,
whiskers on cats,
for wings on songbirds,
bees that buzz...
happy dogs with tails that wag,
smiley monkeys that leap about,
tall giraffes with long, long necks,
elephants with wiggly trunks...
thank you, God,
for creatures all around us!

The birds praise you,
The bees praise you,
And I want to praise you, too!

21

Father God,
I want to say sorry for all the
bad things I have said today,
for all the bad things I have done today,
and to say sorry if I have made anyone sad today.

Father God,
I'm sorry
I got cross today.
I'm sorry
I didn't want
to share today.
I'm sorry
I was unkind today.

23

Praise God,
who gives the sun
and rain,
and swells the grain,
that makes our bread
and keeps us fed

24

Thank you, God,
for a good harvest.
Thank you for food to eat,
some to keep, and some to share.

Be near me,
Lord Jesus,
I ask you to stay
Close by me forever
And love me I pray.
Bless all the dear children
In your tender care
And take us to heaven
To live with you there.

Now I lay me down to sleep,
I pray the Lord my soul to keep:
May God guard me through the night
And wake me with the morning light.

27

God bless all those
that I love;
God bless all those
that love me;
God bless all those
that love those that I love
And all those that love those
that love me.

May the Lord bless us and watch over us. May the Lord make his light shine on us and look after us. May the Lord be kind to us and give us peace; and the blessing of God the Father, Son, and Holy Spirit, be with us and remain with us now and every day.

Published in the UK by
Scamp Publishing
www.scamp-publishing.com

ISBN 978-1-83845-3473

First edition 2011
This edition 2021

Publishing Director: Annette Reynolds
Art Director: Gerald Rogers
Pre-production Manager: GingerPromo, Kev Holt

Printed and bound in China